# The Earth
# and the Stars

*By Richard Whittingham and Barbara Brooks*
*Illustrated by George Suyeoka*

*Created by* SYSTEMS FOR EDUCATION, Inc., *Chicago*
*Published by* THE SOUTHWESTERN COMPANY, *Nashville*

# CONTENTS

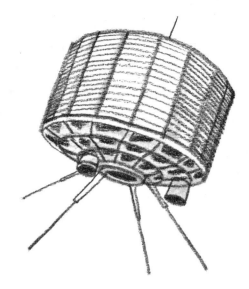

# The Earth and the Sky

DAVID STOOD ON the sidewalk and looked up at the sky. It was a clear night. The sky seemed filled with thousands of blinking stars. He also saw a bright, full moon, which seemed much larger than any of the stars.

David heard footsteps on the sidewalk. He turned quickly. It was his father.

"You've been out here a long time," his father said. "What are you looking at?"

"Just the stars," David said. "There sure are a lot of them."

"How about that light over there?" his father asked.

"That's not a star or a planet. That's a satellite," David answered.

"Right! It orbits around the earth just as the moon does," his father said.

"We have a lot of satellites up there," David said.

"And tonight, there really is a man on the moon," his father said. "Not like the old story of the man *in* the moon. We used to say that because the moon sometimes looked like a face. But today a man from earth actually landed on the moon."

David and his father both stared at the round full moon. They wondered what exciting things the astronaut might be doing up there.

At the same time as David and his father were looking at the moon, the astronaut was looking back at the earth. He could see the outlines of continents and oceans. The earth looked very big and beautiful.

The astronaut wished that everyone on earth could see what their world looked like from the moon. Then they would know what a beautiful place it was. They would appreciate the mountains and the valleys, the islands, the oceans, the lakes and the rivers. The astronaut thought about how much there is to learn just about things on earth. And there is even more to learn about outer space. Then he went back to his work. And, on earth, David and his father walked back into their house.

# When the Earth Was Young

FROM FAR OUT IN SPACE, the earth looks like a blue-green ball. The miles and miles of blue-green ocean make the land part seem small. Actually, the land on which we live and build cities *is* very small. About three-fourths of the earth is covered by water. Land takes up only one quarter of the earth.

Billions of years before there were people or plants or animals on earth, the earth was completely covered by water. Scientists think that the earth remained one great big ocean for many millions of years. Eventually, the first tiny living things appeared in this huge sea.

There were often violent thunderstorms when the earth was young. It would rain for weeks or months at a time. The air was always warm and wet.

Then, over millions of years, the earth slowly changed. Very likely there were great earthquakes and violent volcanoes. No one knows exactly what happened, but very slowly, land rose above the surface of the sea.

The first land was probably not very pleasant. It was swampy and muddy. There were tremendous earthquakes and tidal waves. Volcanoes erupted in many places, and boiling lava poured over the land.

Scientists think that when land finally emerged from the sea, it was not shaped like the land on earth today. Many scientists think that the first land was one big chunk. They have given this first big continent a name— Gondwanaland.

But the earth's top layer, or *crust*, was still very restless. In one especially big earthquake, perhaps, this huge piece of land broke apart in its weakest places. Very slowly, over many, many centuries, large chunks of land floated off from each other. Two large chunks joined by a narrow strip floated to the west, and became North and South America. The biggest chunk broke into three not-quite-separate pieces and floated to the East. It became Europe, Asia and Africa. A very large piece floated up and attached itself to the lower part of Asia, becoming the peninsula of India. Some scientists think this piece bumped the Asian coastline so hard that it pushed up land to form the tall Himalaya mountains.

Scientists have tried very hard to find out if this is really how the continents were formed. The best clue is the *shape* of the continents. The bulge of Africa seems to fit very well into the hollow of the Caribbean Sea between North and South America. And the bulge of South America looks as it it would fit into Africa's hollow just like a piece in a jigsaw puzzle.

This idea about how the continents were formed is called "continental drift." Not all scientists think it is true. But in some way, the land on earth came to look as it does today. A narrow land bridge connects the continents of North and South America. Europe, Asia, and Africa are connected, too. Only a mountain range called the Urals marks the boundary between Europe and Asia.

No matter how it happened, the lands of the earth were divided into definite parts, all quite different. Today many things make these land masses, or *continents*, very different from each other.

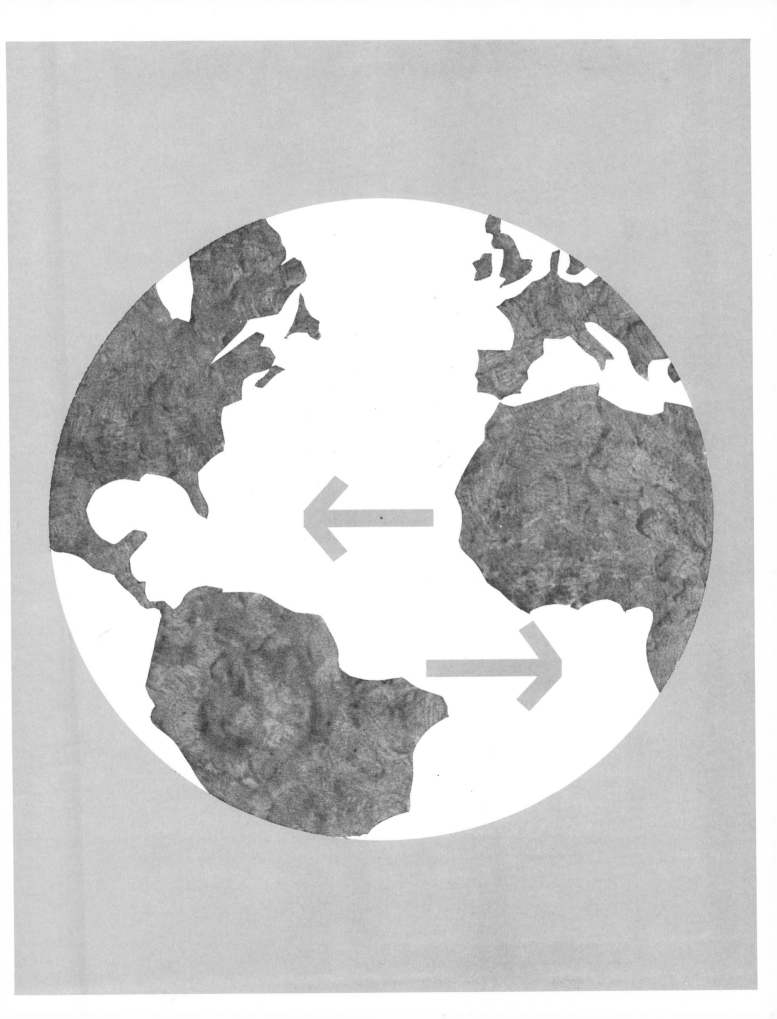

# The Continents

ASIA IS THE BIGGEST continent on earth. Nearly half of all the people in the world live there. The name *Asia* makes most people think of rice and chop suey and pagodas and people who have yellow-brown skins and eat with chopsticks. But Asia is so big that these things are true about only some parts of it.

China has more people than any other country in the world. More than 700 million people live there! In the north, the land of China is cold and dry and hilly. In the south there is hot, wet land, called *padi*, where people grow rice. China has some large cities with factories and stores and large buildings, but most of its people still live and work on farms.

Another large country of Asia is India. It is the big triangular peninsula on the southern part of the continent. India also has many millions of people, who belong to a different race than the Chinese and Japanese and other yellow-skinned Asian peoples.

The other very important country in Asia is Japan. It is on several small islands near the mainland of the continent. The Japanese must use every inch of their land, either to grow food or to make products that they can sell to other countries.

A kind of "land bridge" of many small countries and kingdoms connects the continents of Asia and Africa. These countries are often called "the Middle East." Their people are neither Asian nor African. Most are Arabs. The Middle East is mostly a land of low, flat deserts. There are only a few large cities, like Baghdad in Iraq, Damascus in Syria, Tehran in Iran, Tel Aviv in Israel, and Beirut in Lebanon.

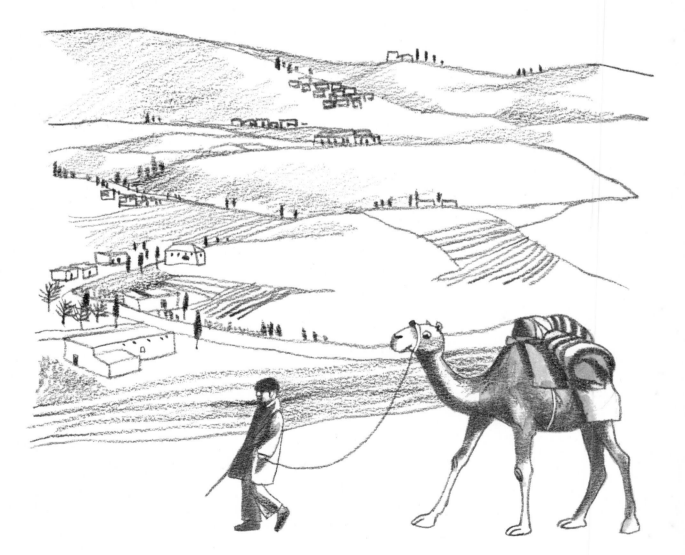

Away from the seacoasts where most cities are, *Africa* has not changed much since ancient times. The countries of central Africa are very near the Equator, and so are hot most of the time. There are thick green rain forests where trees and ferns grow tall enough to block out the sunlight. Wild animals, bright-colored birds, and humming insects live in those jungles. Few people live here. Their small villages, with grass-roofed huts, are built beside the slow-moving rivers.

At the edges of the jungle are miles and miles of broad grasslands. There are no towns or roads here. Hundreds of giraffes, zebras and other animals roam these plains.

North Africa is very different from the steamy jungles and grasslands. Here there is desert, as far as you can see.

Though it is one of the smallest continents, *Europe* has been one of the most important in the history of the world. After the great civilizations of Asia and the Middle East grew less important, Europe became the most powerful part of the world.

Most of the Mediterranean countries—Italy, Greece, Spain, and Portugal—are *peninsulas*. Water surrounds them on three sides. They are warm much of the time, but can be cool and rainy in the mountains and during the winter.

Furthest north in Europe are Sweden, Norway, and Denmark—the countries called *Scandinavia*—and Finland. The northern parts reach all the way to the Arctic. In summer, the "Midnight Sun" shines nearly all night long. Some parts of Scandinavia have steep mountains running down to the sea, with beautiful inlets called *fiords*.

The two largest countries in western Europe are France and Germany. They both have many different kinds of land and people—small farms, little towns, busy cities, thick forests, rugged mountains, and flat

farmland. The famous Alps mountains are in the center of Europe, mostly in the tiny country of Switzerland.

Eastern Europe includes the countries of Poland, Czechoslovakia, Hungary, Yugoslavia, and the eastern part of Germany. This part of Europe has rugged mountains, long rivers, and beautiful old cities like Budapest, Warsaw, and Prague.

The Soviet Union is both the easternmost country in Europe and the westernmost country in Asia. It has more land than any other country in the world. Because it is so big, Russia has many different kinds of lands and people. It is a mixture of Asian and European ways.

In the 1400's the countries of Europe were rich and powerful. But the European kings wanted two things more—more land to rule over, and a better way to get to Asia. From Spain, Portugal, and England, explorers set out across the Atlantic ocean.

The land they found stretched all the way from the cold Arctic in the north to the cold Antarctic in the south.

In between were hot tropical lands, wide warm prairies, and cold mountains. There were two great continents — North and South America.

The western edge of *South America* is edged with the steep Andes mountains. There are many towns and cities in the warm, narrow strip of land between the mountains and the sea. On the eastern side of the mountains, much of the land is hot and tropical.

In some ways, central South America is like central Africa with thick green jungles and slow-moving rivers. Birds and monkeys skitter through the trees. The Amazon, the longest river in the world, runs through the heart of Brazil, the largest country in South America. Practically no one except the Indians who live there has explored this land.

Argentina, to the south, is the other large country. Its central plains are grasslands called *pampas*, where *gauchos* herd cattle like cowboys do in the United States.

Six small tropical countries make up the land bridge of Central America which connects South America to North America. These countries are warm all year

round, and bananas, palm trees, and colorful fruits and plants grow there. Across the narrowest part of Panama runs the famous Panama Canal.

*North America* has three countries—Canada, Mexico, and the United States. These neighbors are quite different from each other.

Mexico is more like South America, because they both were conquered and settled by Spanish soldiers. Like the United States, it had a revolution and became an independent country. A mountain range, the Sierra Madre, runs down its western coast, and in the mountains it is cool and dry. But the parts of Mexico on the seacoast—both on the east and the west—are tropical. Other parts are hot but very dry.

Canada is the largest country in the New World. It is much bigger than the United States; only Russia has more land. The northern parts of Canada stretch all the way to the Arctic. Only Eskimos live there. Other parts of western and northern Canada have very few people and practically no large towns. There are miles and miles of wheat fields and prairies in southern Canada.

Finally, there is the center of the North American continent—the United States. Along the eastern shore is a plain where the first settlers from England, Holland, and Sweden settled. The 13 colonies that became "united states" began here in the 1600's.

Next comes a sharp ridge of mountains that runs from Maine to Georgia. West of the mountains the country flattens out. There are rolling hills and flat prairies all the way to Colorado. In the plains states there are farms where corn and wheat and vegetables grow. There are dairy farms too.

The Rocky Mountains rise up near the western shore of the United States. The West has many other mountain ranges too. The United States, like any large country, has many different kinds of land. Some places are hot and tropical. Others are cool most of the year, with cold snowy winters.

But the United States probably has more different kinds of *people* than most other countries. They have come from Europe, from Asia, from Africa, and even from South America. People from all continents came to build this country in the New World.

# Island Worlds

ISLANDS ARE A KIND of small world by themselves. There is water all around an island — a river, a lake, or an ocean. The only way you can get to an island is by a boat, or an airplane, or sometimes a long bridge.

There are many islands all over the world, both big and small. Some are just large enough for a few trees. But others can hold millions of people and many busy streets full of houses, cars, and skyscrapers. Much of New York City is on three islands — Manhattan, Staten, and Long Islands. Venice in Italy is on so many islands that its streets are mostly canals! The island cities of

Hong Kong and Singapore, off the coast of Asia, are large seaports.

Some islands are so big that they can hold *many* big cities and many people. They are countries all by themselves. The British Isles are two big islands off the continent of Europe. One contains the countries of England, Scotland, and Wales. The other is Ireland.

Japan is a country built on islands that were once the tops of mountains. The four main islands are Honshu, Kyushu, Hokkaido, and Shikoku.

Many islands are rocky and mountainous. These are actually the *tops* of old mountains or volcanoes that sank into the sea, so that nothing shows above the water except the peaks. This is why many islands are long chains, like a string of beads. They are old mountain ranges.

The fiftieth state of the United States, Hawaii, is a chain of nine beautiful green islands that were once the peaks of volcanoes. Other volcanoes in the islands are still active.


## OCEANIA

Between Australia and Southeast Asia, the southern Pacific ocean is so full of islands that it is sometimes called the "continent of Oceania." Once upon a time, millions of years ago, all this land was much higher, and a mountainous land bridge joined Australia to the continent. Then the land shifted and sank. The ocean flowed over much of the land, leaving the peaks and high places as dots of green land in the sea.

The huge jungle islands of Borneo, Java, Sumatra, and New Guinea were some of the largest parts left above water. Farther west are the three groups of islands called Polynesia, Micronesia, and Melanesia, separated by hundreds of miles of water. Famous islands like Samoa and Tahiti are here. They are the homes of the best sailors and navigators in the world — the Polynesians. Thousands of years before anyone in Europe or Africa had the courage to sail more than a few miles from shore, Polynesian sailors in huge outrigger canoes were sailing from island to island. They had no maps and no compasses, but they steered by the stars. Finally, several great canoes sailed most of the way across the Pacific, and the Polynesians became the first settlers of Hawaii.

At the southern tip of the watery continent of Oceania is the biggest island in the world — Australia. It is so large that it is usually listed in books as a continent. If you look for Australia on the globe, you can understand why people sometimes call it "Down Under."

Most of the other important islands of the world are fairly near something else. But Australia has been separated from Asia by the ocean for millions of years. So its plants and animals grew up to be quite a bit different from those in the lands closer together.

Australia has the *kangaroo*, who carries its babies in a pouch like an apron pocket. There's the *koala*, who lives in eucalyptus trees and looks very much like a teddy bear. Other Australian animals are just as unusual as their names — wombats, wallabies, dingos, and the duck-billed platypus! And these strange creatures live nowhere else in the world except Australia. (And in the zoo!)

Most of the people in Australia live near the coast in large cities like Melbourne, Sydney, and Brisbane. Other settlers live on flat plains where sheep or cattle graze on hundreds of miles of empty land. Ranches in Australia are so far apart that nearly everyone travels by airplane. Even doctors and nurses sometimes visit their patients by plane.

# Granite, Glaciers, and Geology

SOME PARTS OF THE WORLD are flat, dry, sandy deserts. Others are rocky and mountainous. Still others are wide, rolling prairies where long grasses grow. The men who study all these different land shapes are called *geologists*. The study of rocks and earth and how mountains and prairies and valleys are formed is called *geology*.

Geologists try to find out why there are mountains in some places and flat plains in others, why lakes and rivers are where they are, and what forces move the earth.

The young earth, millions of years ago, was very restless. There were earthquakes and landslides. Some-

times parts of the rock would be squeezed and folded together, just like a piece of soft wool folded over and over. A long fold of land might make a new mountain range in what had been a prairie.

Geologists have figured out which mountain ranges are "new" and which ones are "old." Probably the oldest mountains in the United States are the Appalachians and the Smokies and other small mountain ranges near the Atlantic ocean. The newest mountains are the Rocky Mountains in Colorado and Montana.

Old mountains are more *weathered*. That word means what it sounds like: storm and winds and rain and dust and all kinds of weather have worn away parts of the rocks of the mountains. Old mountains are lower. Their tops are round, not peaked and jagged. Often they are covered by trees and grass.

New mountains are higher and not so worn down. They have jagged, rocky peaks. Trees seldom grow on these peaks, and snow covers the highest ones all year.

The other great forces that build mountains are deep inside the earth itself. The earth is not a solid ball of soil and rocks and pebbles and boulders. Deep in the earth — deeper than the deepest parts of the sea — the earth is not solid at all. It is so unbelievably hot there that rocks melt! They become sticky, like thick taffy. And they are red hot.

Near the surface of the earth there are sometimes weak spots. In some places the earth's crust is thin. Sometimes the earth slides, and causes earthquakes. Whenever anything happens that makes it possible for the red-hot underground rocks to spurt out, a volcano is formed. Red-hot, liquid rock, called *lava*, flows from a crack in the earth. Sometimes there are explosions, and rocks are tossed high into the air. Ashes, rocks, and lava build up a cone-shaped mountain. Many mountains of today are old volcanoes that do not erupt any more. The Cascade range near the Pacific coast in California is made of old volcanoes.

Volcanoes still erupt in many parts of the world. During our century, several large volcanoes have erupted. Whole cities have been buried by ashes and lava. Many thousands of people have been killed. When Krakatoa, a volcano in Indonesia, erupted in 1883, it killed 36,000 people. The sound of the explosion was heard 3,000 miles away. So much ash and dirt were thrown into the air that there were colorful sunsets all over the world for a year afterward.

One of the most famous volcanoes—Mt. Vesuvius—erupted almost 1900 years ago. It completely buried two little towns, Pompeii and Herculaneum, with ash and soot and lava. People eventually forgot that the towns had ever existed. When the towns were discovered many years afterward, they were almost exactly the way they had been when Vesuvius blew up. Dishes were sitting on the tables in houses. Bread was on the counters in the bakery. The eruption of Vesuvius had stopped everything in just a few minutes.

Only a few volcanoes are building mountains today. But when the earth was younger, millions of years ago, there were many of these fiery mountains. They built mountain ranges and islands all over the world.

## THE CHANGING SURFACE OF EARTH

Volcanoes and earthquakes change the surface of the earth. Many other forces also change the land so that it looks the way it does. Water and weather do much to change the land. After mountains are built, running water carves them into hills and valleys. The Grand Canyon is miles and miles of colorful rock carved into a canyon that is more than a mile deep. At the bottom of the canyon is the tiny Colorado river. Though it is

30

hard to believe, that little river carved the huge canyon out of flat prairie land.

Other rivers, like the Mississippi, pick up dirt and rocks from along their banks and carry them downstream. At the mouths of the rivers, the dirt drops to the bottom, and new land called a *delta* is built.

Sometimes running water and falling water do great damage. They carry away the land where plants grow, and cut deep gullies. When wind and water ruin the land, the damage is called *erosion*.

Most of the water that changes the earth is running water—falling rain and the water that runs in creeks and rivers. But several million years ago, the earth had a long, long winter. Much of the water on earth froze, and became great flat sheets of ice called *glaciers*. Those long-ago glaciers moved mountains, leveled prairies, and dug giant lakes.

The glaciers in North America drifted slowly down from northern Canada. They covered nearly all of the northern half of the United States, as far south as what is now southern Illinois. These glaciers were huge sheets of ice, stretching for hundreds of miles, and almost a mile thick. They slid very slowly across the land.

The glaciers flattened out the flat prairies of the Dakotas, and the rolling plains country in Iowa and Illinois and Minnesota. As the glaciers melted, water filled five of the biggest ditches it had scooped out. These are the five Great Lakes. The glaciers made hundreds of smaller lakes, too.

At the edges of the glaciers the ice melted a little. The rocks and earth that the glaciers scooped off fell to the ground and formed ridges and oddly shaped hills. Giant boulders were dropped in fields many miles from where they had been picked up.

Compared with the other things that have changed the earth, glaciers came only a short time ago. Geologists think the last ones melted back about 11,000 years ago. Most of the other things geologists study happened millions and billions of years ago. So 11,000 years ago is practically yesterday!

There are still a few glaciers and ice sheets in the world today. Antarctica, the land around the South Pole, is covered by a great ice sheet ten miles thick in places. There are ice sheets near the North Pole, too. And there are smaller valley glaciers in many of the mountains of the world. They are still at work carving mountains.

Geologists think that we are just at the end of a great Ice Age. Unless something very unusual happens to the world's weather, there will not be another Ice Age for thousands of years. But the forces that change the land are still at work. The earth's surface is slowly changing all the time.

# Water, Wind, and Weather

EVERYONE ON EARTH lives at the bottom of a great "sea" of air—the atmosphere around the earth. The atmosphere is made up of oxygen, other gases, little specks of dust—and *water*. Only a very little bit of all the water in the world is in the atmosphere. Most of the water is in the oceans. Yet water in the air is one of the most important things in giving us the kind of weather we have.

Sometimes the air loses a lot of its water, and then *rain* or *snow* falls. Sometimes the water collects around little specks of dust in the air and makes *clouds*.

Water from lakes, rivers, and oceans—and even little puddles—is constantly *evaporating*. It becomes *water vapor* and rises into the air. The air carries this water vapor to somewhere else. When the water vapor *condenses*, or turns back into water, it may fall as rain. It may freeze, and then it falls as snow. The rainfall and melting snow soak into the ground, or flow into rivers and creeks that carry them back to the lakes and oceans. There the water evaporates again, and rises into the air.

Weathermen have special names for the different kinds of clouds we see in the sky. The big piles of cottony clouds that move across the summer sky are called *cumulus*. Flat, streaky layers of clouds are called *stratus*. The high, wispy bits of clouds are named *cirrus*. These feathery clouds are so high in the sky that they are frozen. Cirrus clouds are made of ice crystals, not water droplets.

One kind of cumulus cloud almost always means a storm is coming. It is a high, flat-topped pile of clouds that seems to sit right on the horizon and tower into the sky. Sometimes people call such a cloud a *thunderhead*.

Another thing that is important in giving us the kind of weather we have is *wind*. Wind is air that is moving very fast. The air is always moving, no matter how quiet it may seem.

Winds are named for *where* they blow from most of the time. At the far north and far south, around the North and South Poles, the *polar winds* blow. They are icy cold, because they come from lands where there is ice and snow all year round. When cold, cold air blows from the polar zones, nearby parts of the world will have cold weather.

Around the Equator are two belts of *trade winds*. These are hot, dry winds that blow toward the Equator.

The winds that blow most of the time around the central areas of earth's two hemispheres are very important because they affect such a large part of the world. They are called *prevailing winds* because they blow in one direction most of the time. The prevailing winds are caused by the earth's spinning round and round, once each day.

In the northern hemisphere, the lands north of the Equator, the prevailing winds are *westerlies*. They blow from west to east. In the southern hemisphere, they are *prevailing easterlies*. They blow from east to west.

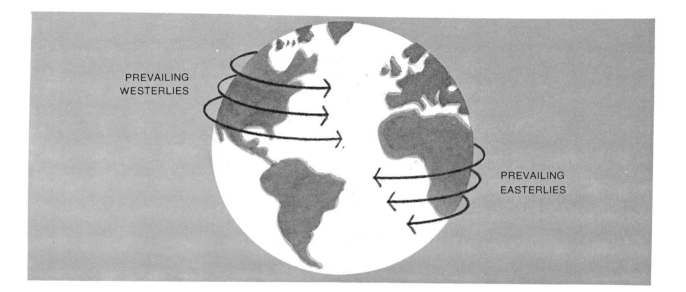

When the prevailing winds blow across huge oceans like the Atlantic or the Pacific, they pick up great amounts of water vapor. By the time they reach the western coasts of the big continents, the winds are very, very wet. As soon as they reach the land, they rise in the air—and drop most of their water as rain. If there are mountains along the coast, nearly all of the water in the air is dropped on the coastward side of the mountain range. The coasts of California, Washington, and Oregon in the United States get much rain brought by prevailing westerlies. So do England and the western shores of Europe.

In the southern hemisphere, it is the east coasts that are very rainy. The jungle of Brazil in South America is tropical rain forest watered by rain from prevailing easterly winds.

When the prevailing winds have blown over the coast areas, they continue inland, but they have very little water left in them. This is why the central parts of very large continents may be fairly dry grasslands or prairies, or even very dry deserts.

Much of the world's weather is caused by *local* winds and masses of warm or cold air that move across the land. Weathermen trace the paths of these air masses when they figure out the weather forecast for the next few days. Have you seen a weatherman on television draw lines and circles on the weather map? These show what storms or air masses are moving toward you.

Some strong storm winds have special names. *Tornadoes* are whirling, funnel-shaped wind clouds that can damage towns and buildings. They usually form in flat prairie country, where there are no hills or trees to break the wind. *Hurricanes* are violent storms that blow off the ocean. They often do great damage to towns near the coast and to ships at sea.

Weathermen use weather balloons to learn about conditions high in the sky, and they use weather satellites to find out where storms are. A weather satellite can take pictures of almost the whole United States, showing exactly where storms are and where they are moving. Weathermen also use instruments to measure temperature and humidity.

The *temperature* reading tells how hot or cold the air is. The thermometer used in the United States measures heat and cold in degrees Fahrenheit. We say that 32 degrees Fahrenheit is freezing temperature—water turns to ice, and water in the air turns to hail or snow. In many other countries, and in most scientific laboratories, a different temperature scale, called Centigrade, is used. On the Centigrade thermometer, zero is the freezing point of water.

*Humidity* is the measure of how much water there is in the air. Warm air can hold much more water than cold air. When the wind hits a mountain range, it is forced higher into the air where it is cooler. Rain falls because the cooler air can no longer hold all its water.

Sometimes on very hot summer days, the air feels as though you could wring it out like a wet sponge. This means that the humidity is very high, probably over 90 per cent. If the humidity goes higher, you can expect rain. A "relative humidity" of 100 per cent means that the air is holding all the water it can. If the temperature drops, the cooler air will not be able to hold so much water, and rain will probably fall.

# What Ancient People
# Thought About Space

THROUGHOUT THE AGES man has wondered about the sky. Cavemen carved pictures of the sun and the stars on the walls of their caves. Some ancient people worshipped the sun as a powerful god. They even built great temples to it, and they offered human sacrifices to the sun. And the stars, some people believed, were stuck to a huge dome. The earth was flat, they thought, and the dome was somehow attached to the ends of the earth.

It has taken men thousands of years to learn what we now know about the heavens. Today, much of what the ancient people thought about space seems ridiculous.

Yet they were trying to understand and explain the fascinating story of the heavens.

Ancient people began to study the sun, moon, stars and planets thousands of years before the birth of Christ. This study is the science we call *astronomy*.

Ancient people tried to explain what they saw in the skies. Some Chinese said that the Milky Way galaxy was steam from the breath of a huge elephant who lay submerged to his neck in the water of the skies. Some Greeks believed that the Milky Way was the main road through heaven. In Egypt, some people said that it was formed by kernels of corn dropped by the goddess Isis.

Ancient people felt that certain groups of stars made pictures in the sky. They named the groups after what the pictures looked like—Taurus the Bull, Aries the Ram, Pisces the Fish. These pictures in the sky are what we call *constellations*.

Ancient people used the stars and constellations to guide them at night. And they believed that the stars and constellations were responsible for much of what happened on Earth. Any strange event in the sky frightened them. A comet or a meteor was viewed with great fear by the people. A planet entering a certain constellation would suggest that some fearful or disastrous event was to take place on Earth.

These beliefs remained for thousands of years. In the year 1524, over 30 years after America was discovered, people all over the civilized world saw a terrible sign in the skies. Three planets—Mars, Jupiter and Saturn—came together in the constellation of Pisces the Fish. People believed this meant a great flood would cover the Earth. Many stopped their normal work and frantically built boats and arks. The flood, of course, never came.

41

The most common belief in ancient times was that the Earth was the center of the universe. In China, however, some astronomers held that the North Star, which we call *Polaris* or Pole Star, was the center. An ancient Greek astronomer named Aristarchus said the Earth revolved around the sun, but few people were willing to accept this idea.

The most famous of the early astronomers was a man named Ptolemy who lived in Egypt over 1,850 years ago. He wrote a book called the *Almagest* in which he "proved" that everything in the heavens revolved around the Earth. For the next 1,400 years, most people believed Ptolemy's idea.

It was not until the great age of astronomers in the 1500's and 1600's that Ptolemy's idea was corrected. Copernicus and Galileo started men on the right track to understanding the universe by explaining that the earth and other planets revolve around the sun. Other great astronomers like Tycho Brahe, Johann Kepler, Isaac Newton and Edmund Halley added still more to our understanding of the heavenly bodies.

# Our Sun

OUR SUN IS a faithful friend. Every morning it rises in the east, often long before we get out of bed. It slowly lights up the sky. The darkness of night disappears.

Even on a cloudy morning when we cannot see the sun at all, it gives off enough light to let us know that it is daytime. We can be absolutely certain that every morning the sun will be there. Our faithful sun has not missed a day since the world began. And it never will as long as our world exists.

The sun really doesn't *rise*. It seems to come up in the east, and to travel slowly across the sky until it passes out of sight in the west each night. What really happens is that the Earth, our planet, is rotating. It is spinning around like a top. In the morning when we first see the sun, the part of the Earth where we live is turning toward the sun. The Earth continues to turn, and gradually the part where we live turns away from the sun. Then we have night. Each 24 hours the sun appears again.

Even thousands of years ago, ancient people knew how important the sun was. Many of them worshipped it as a god. Some Egyptians thought the sun was a bright, fiery ship that sailed across the sky each day, or a great ball of fire pushed by a beetle!

The ancient people of Greece told a story about how hot the sun was. A clever man named Daedalus made two pairs of wings so that he and his son could fly away from their enemies. But his son Icarus was foolish and flew too close to the sun. The sun was so hot that it melted the wax which held his wings on. Poor Icarus fell into the sea.

This story, of course, is a *myth*, a story like a fairy tale. But even if Icarus could fly, he could not fly very close to the sun. The sun is about 93 million miles away from the Earth. If he flew at 60 miles per hour without ever stopping, it would have taken him 177 years to reach the sun.

And the sun is very much hotter than the ancient Greeks thought it was. We think it is hot here on Earth when the temperature reaches 90 degrees. The temperature on the surface of the sun is about 12,000 degrees. And inside the sun at its *core*, the temperature is over 20 million degrees.

If the sun is so hot, why doesn't it just burn up? After all, it is much hotter than any fire or heat here on Earth.

It is important to understand that the sun is not a ball of fire, although it may look like one. Also, the sun is not solid like the Earth or the moon. It is made up of

gases. One type of gas on the sun is *hydrogen*. Through a nuclear reaction, hydrogen gas changes into helium gas. When this happens tremendous heat is created. This nuclear reaction goes on all the time, and so the sun remains a glowing ball of intense heat.

The sun is a place of tremendous action too. Violent explosions shake its surface. From deep inside the sun, hot gases called *flares* burst through the sun's surface. Streams of hot gases leap out like great torches. Some of these streamers reach out a hundred thousand miles and then fall back into the sun. Cooler gases form dark spots on the sun, which are called *sunspots*. Sunspots may last only a few hours or for as long as two months. Their temperature is much lower than the area around them.

Like all of the other stars, the sun is moving. In fact, nothing in the universe is standing still. The sun rotates on its own axis. At the same time, it moves through space carrying the Earth and the other planets right along with it.

Our sun is a star, like many of the other stars in the sky. It only looks different, because it is so much closer to us. The other stars are billions of miles farther away. Most of them are so far away we cannot even see them without a telescope. But most of them are suns, much like our sun. They, too, produce heat, light and energy.

Our sun is very large. More than one million planets the size of our Earth would fit inside it. Yet our sun is only an average-size star. There are many stars which are much brighter. Others are hundreds of times larger. Still, to us, it is the most important star in the universe.

# Our Moon

THE ASTRONAUT standing on the moon was the first human being ever to get there. In fact, he was the first man to leave the Earth and land on another world in outer space. When he landed on the moon, there was no one to welcome him. His space craft had no airport or space platform on which to land. He could see no grass or trees, no animals or buildings, no lakes or rivers. There were only rocks and dust.

The astronaut, of course, was not surprised. He knew before he left the Earth that there were no living things and no water on the moon. *Astronomers* and other

47

scientists had taught him many things about what the moon would be like.

Men had been studying the moon for hundreds of years. The fact that the moon travels around the Earth was discovered by an Italian astronomer named Galileo Galilei, who lived about 350 years ago.

How did Galileo discover this amazing fact? He built a small telescope, and with it he was able to look out into space and see things that no man had ever seen before. With his telescope he was able to see that the planet Jupiter had four moons. He found that those moons were revolving around Jupiter. Then he was able to determine that *our* moon was revolving around *our* planet Earth. Later, more powerful telescopes were developed, and it was discovered that Jupiter actually has 12 moons, some of them as big or even bigger than our moon.

The telescope was a wonderful invention. With it, man could study much more closely all of the heavenly bodies—the moon, planets, the sun and the stars. Telescopes allow us to see things which we could not see with just our eyes. Scientists through the years have created better and better telescopes. The telescopes scientists use today are much better than the one that Galileo used.

Another thing that helped the astronaut learn more about the moon was the invention of rockets and missiles. With these powerful vehicles, men launched satellites around the Earth. Later spacecraft were built that could go even farther and orbit the moon. And finally there were rockets which could safely land on the moon. Scientists learned how to take close-up pictures and gather other information about the moon.

With the telescope and other wonderful inventions, men learned exactly how far away the moon was and how large it was. The astronaut knew that the moon is usually about 238,000 miles from the Earth. He also knew that at certain times it is over 253,000 miles away. At other times it is closer, only a little over 221,000 miles away. A trip to the moon would be like traveling from New York to San Francisco 80 times without stopping.

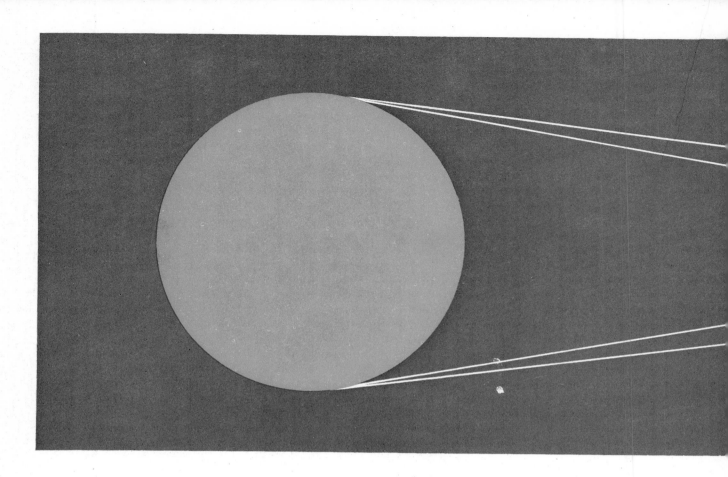

The astronaut also knew that the moon was different from the Earth in other ways. On the moon there are only mountains, craters and valleys. They are covered with rocks and dust.

The moon has no water and no air. The air that surrounds our Earth—the same air we breathe—is called our *atmosphere*. The moon has no atmosphere. Because it has no atmosphere, the moon has no clouds, no wind, and no rain or snow. Because there is no air on the moon, the astronaut has to wear a helmet which completely covers his head and a space suit which covers his body. Air is pumped into the helmet from tanks brought from Earth so he can breathe.

Each "day" on the moon is two weeks long, and each "night" lasts two weeks. During the daylight time, the temperature is very hot, usually about 214 degrees,

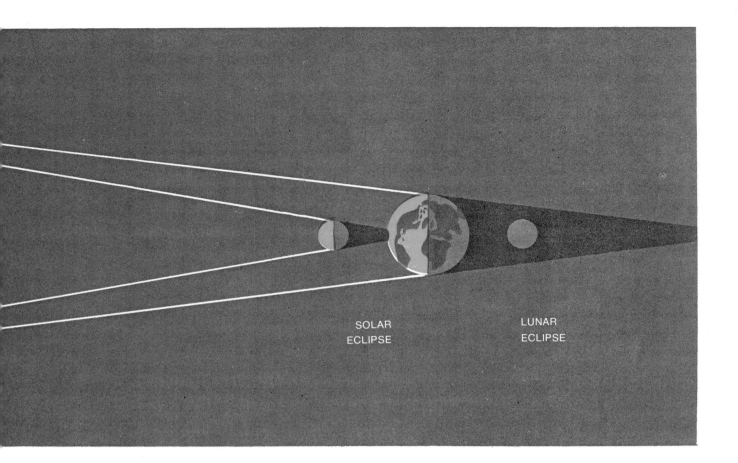

SOLAR
ECLIPSE

LUNAR
ECLIPSE

which is hot enough to boil water. At night it turns very cold, and the temperature is sometimes 243 degrees below zero. Scientists knew about these very hot and cold temperatures on the moon. That is why they developed a special space suit for the astronaut. Otherwise he could not live on the moon.

To us on Earth the moon always seems to be changing its shape. Sometimes we see a round full moon, other times only a half-moon, and sometimes only a sliver of a moon. There are nights when we can see no moon at all.

Half of the moon is always lighted by the sun, but we do not always see all of the lighted half. How much of the lighted half we see depends on where the moon is in its orbit around the Earth.

As it travels around the Earth, the moon sometimes passes between the sun and the Earth and blots out the light of the sun. This is called a *solar eclipse*. Ancient peoples used to be terrified when a solar eclipse occurred. There are times, too, when the moon is on the other side of the Earth. Then, the Earth is between the sun and the moon, and the Earth blocks off the light from the sun. When this happens the Earth casts its shadow across the moon, causing a *lunar eclipse*.

The moon is certainly not a pleasant place to visit. Why then do people go to all the trouble of sending astronauts there? There are really many reasons.

For one thing, there may be valuable minerals on the moon, like gold, uranium, iron or nickel. Another reason is that we can study the stars and planets much more easily from the moon because the moon has no atmosphere. Telescopes on the moon would give us much clearer views of the stars and planets than they do from Earth. Also, from the moon, we would probably be able to predict the weather on Earth much better. From the moon it would be possible to see giant storms taking shape halfway around the world.

The most exciting thing about being able to reach the moon is that we could build a space station there. From this space station, space ships could be launched to explore other planets. The moon will be our first stop in exploring the universe.

# The Planets

"THE EARTH IS NOT the center of the universe," said the famous astronomer Nicolas Copernicus. "We have been wrong. It is really the Earth that revolves around the sun."

Copernicus suggested this astonishing idea in the early 1500's. For thousands of years people had believed that everything in the heavens revolved around the Earth. Copernicus knew that people were not ready to accept his startling idea, which would upset many religious beliefs. So he wrote it in a book that he did not allow to be published until after his death.

Copernicus was right, of course, about people not being ready to believe him. Many years would pass before people would accept his idea.

Today, we know that the Earth is only one of nine planets which all revolve around our sun. We call the sun and the planets that go around it our *solar system*. Our solar system includes the sun and everything that revolves around it—planets, moons, comets, meteors and asteroids. But the planets are the most important.

On a clear night, we can sometimes see some of the planets. Planets reflect light from our sun, just as the moon does. Because the planets are much nearer to us than any of the stars, they usually look bigger and brighter than the stars.

We know of nine planets in our solar system. There may be others which have not yet been located. In fact, the last planet to be discovered, Pluto, was not found until 1930.

The planets do not move around the sun in a perfect circle. They move in an *ellipse*, which is sort of a stretched-out circle.

54

Copernicus said that in addition to traveling around the sun, each planet also turns on its own *axis*. This is another way of saying that each planet spins like a top as it moves around the sun.

Why do the planets stay in their orbits around the sun? Why don't they fly off into space? A famous English astronomer named Isaac Newton found the explanation. It is a force we call *gravity*. Newton said that everything is pulled toward something else. The bigger and closer an object is, the more power it has in drawing things toward it. The Earth is the biggest and closest thing to us who live on it. Therefore, it pulls us toward it. We do not float off into space. We throw a ball into the air and it falls back to Earth. It is drawn back by the force of gravity.

In our solar system, the biggest object is the sun. It draws the Earth and all the other planets toward it. Why aren't we pulled into the sun, then? The answer is because we are whirling around the sun.

If you tie a ball on a string and swing it around in a circle, it stays in the air and feels as if it is trying to pull away from you. This pulling-away feeling is called *centrifugal* force. The Earth and the planets are swinging around the sun much like balls on the ends of strings. Gravity— the pulling-in power of the sun—keeps the planets from whirling off into space. Centrifugal force—the pulling-away power of the whirling planets—keeps the planets from being drawn into the sun. The two forces work against each other to keep us orbiting around the sun.

*Mercury*, the planet closest to the sun, is also one of the smallest. It takes Mercury only 88 days to make a complete orbit around the sun. That means Mercury's

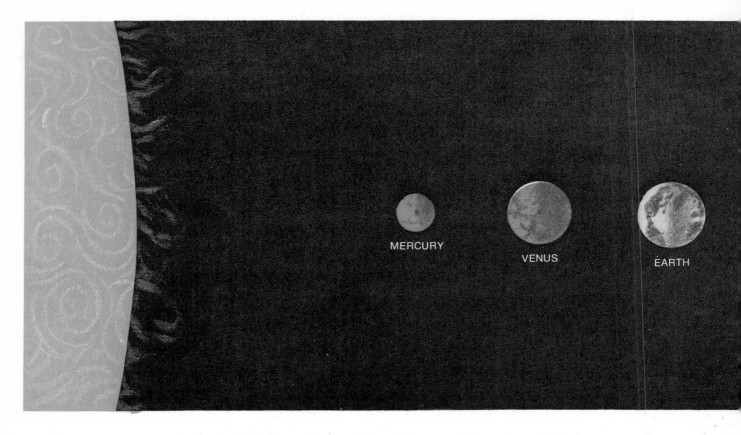

MERCURY

VENUS

EARTH

year is only 88 days long. But Mercury makes only one turn on its axis every 88 days. Therefore, one side of Mercury is always facing the sun. It is tremendously hot. Scientists think it is about 770 degrees on the daylight side of Mercury. The other side is always facing away from the sun. It is always very cold, more than 200 degrees below zero.

*Venus* is the planet closest to the Earth. At one point in its orbit, it is only 25 million miles from the Earth. Venus is about the same size as the Earth, and takes 225 days to orbit the sun. Venus is surrounded by thick clouds that make it impossible to see the planet. Space ships have sent back word that Venus is also very hot — about 500 degrees. This planet is among the brightest and most beautiful sights in the sky.

*Earth* is certainly the most important planet to us. It is our home. Earth is a medium-sized planet. It travels around the sun once in 365 days, which is how we

MARS

JUPITER

determine our year. And it rotates on its axis once every 24 hours (a day). To us, the Earth seems a very big place, but in the universe, it is only a tiny speck.

*Mars* is the next farthest planet out beyond Earth. Mars takes 687 days to revolve around the sun. It has a bright red glow, and can be seen easily from the Earth. Through a telescope, astronomers can see light and dark patches on Mars. It was once thought that the light areas were deserts and the dark areas were seas. But scientists now believe that there is probably no water at all on Mars. Space ships have sent back pictures which seem to show that Mars is a dry, dusty place like the moon.

*Jupiter* is the largest planet, though it is still much smaller than our sun. This giant planet is about 1500 times as big as our Earth, and it has 12 moons! Through a telescope, patches and spots can be seen on Jupiter. Some astronomers think these may be clouds. It takes Jupiter almost 12 of our Earth years to orbit around the sun.

SATURN

URANUS

*Saturn* is one of the most unusual of the planets because it has three rings which encircle it. The rings vary in brightness. They also cast shadows on the planet itself. The rings seem to be made of millions of small meteors or other tiny particles. Each particle is probably no bigger than a small stone. Saturn is the second largest planet in our solar system. Its orbit around the sun takes nearly 30 Earth years.

*Uranus* was not discovered until 1781. It is smaller than Jupiter or Saturn but still much larger than the Earth. Uranus is difficult to see because it is so far away. It takes this planet 84 Earth years to orbit the sun!

*Neptune* cannot be seen without a telescope. It is slightly smaller than Uranus, but is still one of the giant

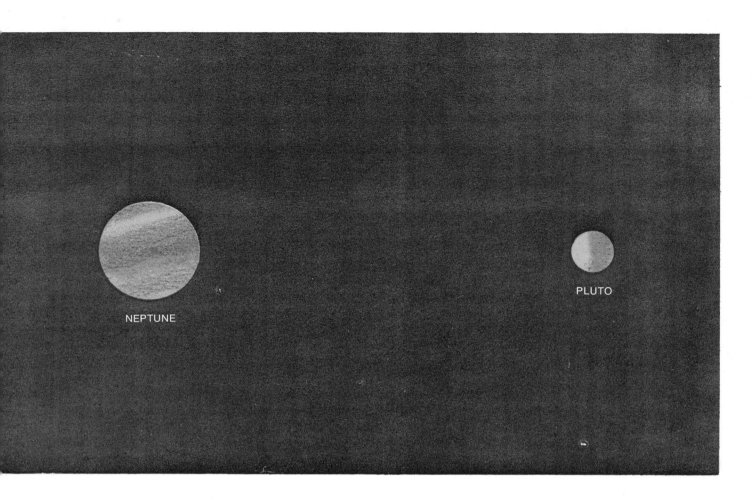

planets. Neptune is tremendously cold because it is so far away from the sun. In fact, the warmest it gets on Neptune is 360 degrees below zero. It takes Neptune 164 Earth years to travel once around the sun.

*Pluto* is the farthest planet we know about. We think it is also the smallest. Pluto was not discovered until 1930. Some scientists believe that it is not a planet at all. They think it is perhaps one of Neptune's moons. Pluto takes over 247 years to orbit the sun. It is a bitterly cold, desolate planet, so far away that we have been able to learn very little about it. Pluto is so far from the Earth that light from it takes over five hours to reach us. If Pluto suddenly blew up, we would not know it on Earth until five hours later.

# Comets, Meteors, and Asteroids

COMETS ARE AMONG the most exciting things in the sky. Some travel swiftly through the sky streaming a bright fiery tail behind them.

Before people knew much about comets, they were afraid of these strange visitors in the heavens. People thought that the appearance of a comet meant some terrible tragedy would happen on Earth. We know today that this is not true at all. A comet is simply another neighbor of ours in space.

Comets usually make a wide orbit around the sun. Their orbit is an *ellipse*, like that of the planets, but

it is much longer. At one end of the comet's orbit is the sun, and at the other end usually one of the large planets like Jupiter or Neptune. As it approaches the sun a comet moves much faster, because the sun's tremendous force of *gravity* pulls it faster.

A comet with a tail is easy to spot. However, most comets do not have tails. As comets approach the sun, some will form a tail. The closer the comet gets to the sun, the longer the tail becomes. Some comet tails are millions of miles long. As the comet passes around the sun and heads back out into space, the tail gets smaller and smaller until it finally disappears.

The tail of a comet always points away from the sun. This is because the pressure from the sun pushes gases and dust away from the head of the comet. The tail is simply the gases and dust trailing behind.

Comets are very light in weight. In fact, the Earth is about a million times heavier than the heaviest comet. No one knows for sure what comets are made of. They are probably loose clumps of gases, dust and small rocks.

One of the most famous comets is Halley's comet. It is named after the astronomer who discovered it, Edmund Halley. It appears in the sky about every 75 years. Some comets, however, appear only every thousand years or more. Halley's comet last was seen from Earth in 1910. It is scheduled to visit the Earth again in 1985 or 1986.

Meteors are another interesting sight in the sky. They are often called "shooting stars" because they make a bright flash, racing across the sky. But they are not stars. Stars do not fall or shoot across the sky.

Meteors are chunks of stone or iron. They vary in size from a tiny speck of dust to large boulders weighing several tons. But all meteors are too small to see when they are in outer space. When a meteor enters the Earth's atmosphere, it becomes tremendously hot as it rushes through the air. The meteor becomes a white-hot glowing ball speeding toward the Earth. The brightest meteors are called *fireballs*. They are so bright they seem to light up the entire sky. If it is a large meteor, small chunks may break off and trail behind it. When this happens, the stream of bright pieces trailing behind the meteor looks like a fireworks display.

After a meteor has fallen to Earth, it is called a *meteorite*. Most meteorites are very small, but a few large ones have been found. The largest was discovered in Africa, and weighed almost 60 tons. Meteor Crater in

Arizona is believed to have been caused by the crash of a meteor. The crater is three-fourths of a mile wide and almost 600 feet deep!

Most meteors burn up completely before they reach the Earth. But still, about 2,000 large meteors strike the Earth each year.

Asteroids are chunks of stone or iron like meteors, but they are much larger. Even though we call them the "little planets," they are much smaller than even the smallest planet. Asteroids come in all shapes and sizes. Some are fairly round like the planets. Others are rugged and resemble a huge boulder. One called *Eros* looks like a giant loaf of bread.

Each asteroid revolves around the sun in its own orbit. Practically all of them are between the orbits of Mars and Jupiter. Only one asteroid, named *Vesta*, can be seen without a telescope. The others are too small and too far away.

We do not know how the asteroids came to be. Some scientists think that they were created at the same time and in the same way as the planets. Others believe that there was once a planet between Mars and Jupiter. This planet either exploded or collided with some other huge body in space. The shattered pieces of planet are what we call asteroids.

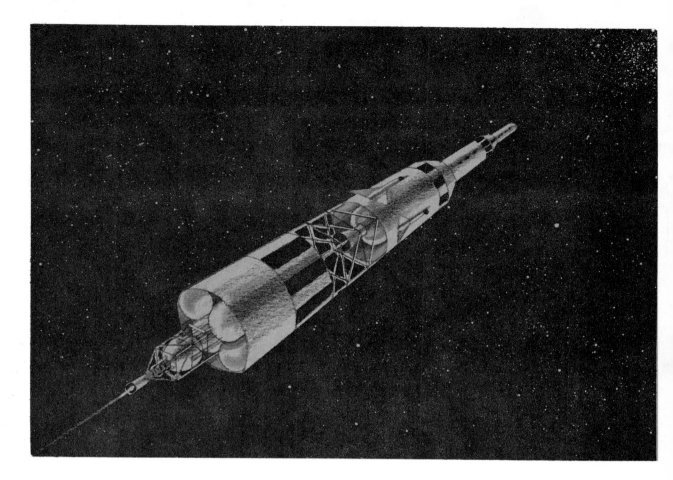

# Among the Stars

SUPPOSE THAT THERE IS LIFE on a planet which revolves around a star far away from the Earth. Suppose someone there wants to send us a letter to tell us that there is life on that planet. He would have to address his letter something like this:

> Mr. David Johnson
> 1516 N. Main Street
> Chicago, Illinois, U. S. A.
> The Earth
> The Solar System
> The Milky Way Galaxy
> The Universe

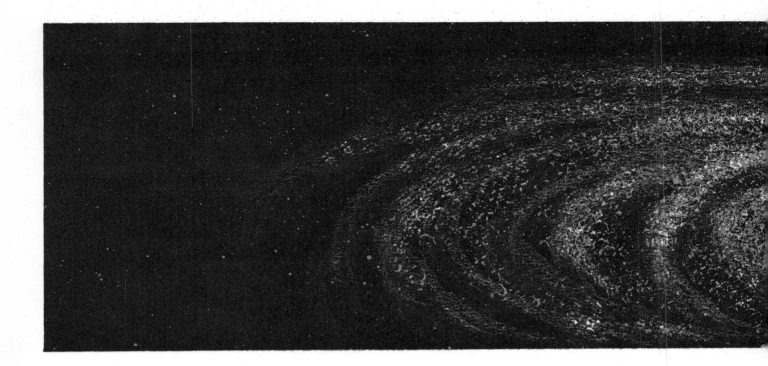

Suppose, too, that the Post Office on his planet can send letters at the speed of light, which is 186,000 miles per second. That means that the letter would travel 16,070,400,000 miles in a day. But even traveling at this incredible rate of speed, the letter would not reach us on Earth for hundreds of millions of *years*. That is how far away some of the stars are from the Earth.

Our sun is a star, too. It looks different from other stars simply because it is so much closer to us. But it is only one of trillions of stars in the sky.

Our sun-star is part of a *system* of stars called a *galaxy*. Our galaxy is known as the Milky Way galaxy because the part of it that we can see from Earth looks like a great milky ribbon spread across the night sky. There are more than a hundred billion stars in our Milky Way galaxy.

If we were able to stand back and look at the whole Milky Way galaxy, it would look like a huge pinwheel. It is flat, like a wheel, but bulging in the center as if it has hubcaps. Two long arms of the pinwheel trail out

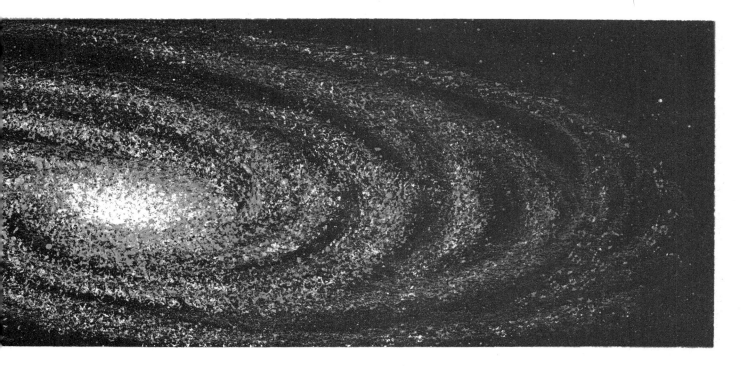

from the center. There are billions of stars in our galaxy, and all of them are constantly in motion. Our galaxy is like a tremendous wheel turning in space.

Our sun is about 35,000 *light years* from the center of the Milky Way galaxy. That means if you were traveling through space at 186,000 miles per second (the speed of light), it would take you 35,000 years to reach the center of our galaxy. Our sun—together with its planets, comets, asteroids, and meteors—is on one of the huge arms streaming out from the center of the galaxy. The distance from one side of the Milky Way galaxy all the way across to the other side is over 80,000 light years.

As huge as our galaxy is, it is by no means the only one in the universe. There are at least a hundred million other galaxies. Probably there are many, many more which we cannot see because our telescopes are not powerful enough. Many of the other galaxies we can see are much larger than ours.

Many stars, too, are larger than our sun, and many are brighter. In fact, our sun is only an average star in size and brightness. Some stars are large enough to put almost half of our solar system inside them.

We can tell about the *heat* of a star by its color. The "hottest" are blue stars and white stars. Average stars are yellow. The coldest stars are red. We also describe stars by their size—these sizes are super-giant, giant, or dwarf. Our sun is yellow, which means it is medium hot, and is classified as a giant star.

Some stars are really *double stars* or *star clusters*. They sometimes look like just a single star. But when we look through a telescope we find that there are two or even more stars. A star cluster may be several stars which are not close together at all, but are simply in the same line of sight. Or it may be several stars which are close together, making up their own system. The most famous star clusters are the Pleiades, sometimes called the Seven Sisters, and the Gemini Twins.

Out among the stars, there are also *nebulae*. These are great clouds of gas. There are different kinds of nebulae. A *planetary nebula* is a huge mass of gas which surrounds a star. There is also a *gaseous nebula*, which is a thin cloud of gas that appears as a bright object in the sky. A *dark nebula*, which looks like a hole in the sky, is really a mass of gases and other material located between us and stars out beyond it. A dark nebula blocks our view of other stars and appears as a dark blot in the sky.

We often think of the stars as only being out at night. The stars, of course, are there all the time. We can see them only at night. During the day the light from our own sun is so bright we cannot see any of the other stars.

Even though our sun is by far the most important star to us on Earth, the other stars are helpful. Travelers for centuries used them to find their way at night. Ships and even airplanes have used stars to help them navigate.

People in the southern hemisphere of Earth do not see the same stars as people in the northern hemisphere. They look out on a different section of the sky, one which people in the northern hemisphere never see. The brightest star in the northern skies is Sirius, but it cannot be seen from Australia or Argentina. On the other hand, the brightest star in the southern skies is Canopus, which cannot be seen in the north. The most famous constellation in that part of the world is the Southern Cross.

# Rockets and Missiles

ALTHOUGH POWERFUL ROCKETS for space exploration are new, man has known how to make simple rockets for hundreds of years.

In the year 1232, the Chinese used rockets in battle. The rockets were attached to sticks and fired from the ground. They were called "arrows of fire."

Over 200 years later, an Italian named Joanes de Fontana designed other rockets for war. His plan was to equip the rockets with rollers or wheels and disguise them as rabbits, fish and birds. They were supposed to roll across the battlefield and terrify the enemy.

About the year 1500, a Chinese named Wan Hoo became the first man to try to use rockets as a form of travel. He gathered 47 of the largest rockets available and attached them to the back of a chair. A kite was placed on each side of the chair. Wan Hoo sat in the chair and signalled his helpers to ignite the 47 rockets. They carefully lit the fuses and then retreated a safe distance. In a huge blast of noise and flame, Wan Hoo and his "rocket-chair" became the first casualty in man's attempt to soar into outer space.

As the years passed, men began to develop better rockets. In the early 1800's a man in Paris named Claude Ruggieri developed small rockets which carried rats and mice into the air. The rockets were equipped with tiny automatic parachutes so that his little passengers could return to Earth safely.

Also in the early 1800's, effective rockets for war were being developed by William Congreve. They were an important weapon for England in the Napoleonic Wars with France and in the War of 1812 against the United States.

It was not until the 1920's, however, that the first real step toward modern rocketry was made. Dr. Robert H. Goddard, an American scientist, developed in 1926 the first rocket which was propelled by a liquid fuel. Before then all rockets had used a solid fuel like gunpowder. Today, most of our powerful rockets use liquid fuels such as liquid hydrogen or oxygen.

Doctor Goddard's work was not easy. It took many years of study, experiments, and tests. Some people laughed at him, others said he was a fake. After one especially noisy test-firing at a farm in Auburn, Massachusetts, many of his neighbors called the police. They thought a plane was on fire and had crashed nearby. Dr. Goddard was called before the state fire marshal. He was asked to discontinue rocket tests in the state. So, Dr. Goddard continued his experiments elsewhere. He finally developed rockets that could soar thousands of feet into the air at speeds over 600 miles an hour.

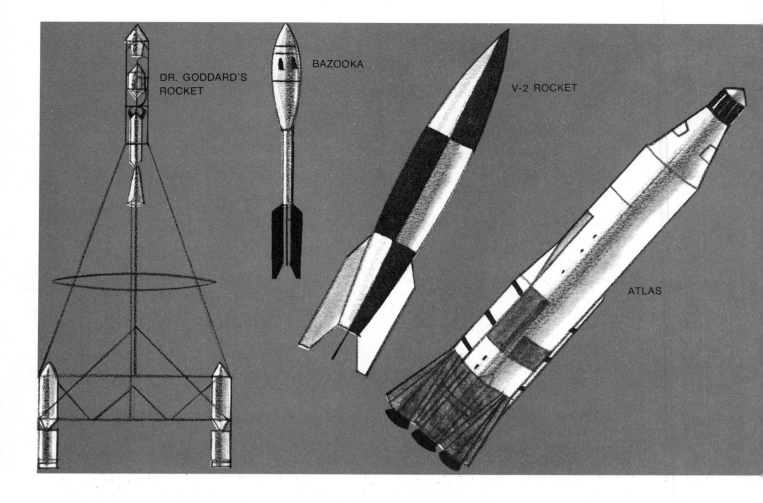

DR. GODDARD'S ROCKET

BAZOOKA

V-2 ROCKET

ATLAS

More advances in rockets came during World War II. The bazooka became an important weapon. With it, foot soldiers could launch a rocket powerful enough to destroy a tank. The Russians used larger rockets fired from launching pads on the ground or from trucks. These rockets helped the Russians defeat the Germans in the fierce battles of Stalingrad and Leningrad.

In Germany, scientists developed the V-2 rocket. This giant rocket could travel over 200 miles. It could travel at 3,000 miles an hour, which was a fantastic rate of speed for the 1940's. The V-2's brought terror and destruction to London during World War II.

In the short period from the end of World War II in 1945 to the 1960's, men made giant strides in the devel-

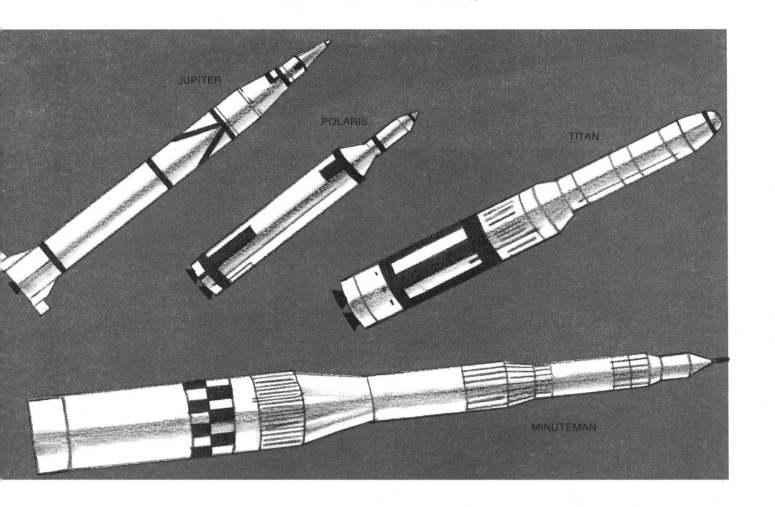

opment of rockets and missiles. In less than 20 years, rocket scientists advanced from the V-2 rocket which could travel 200 miles to rockets which could soar out past many of the planets.

Missiles became an important part of the U.S. national defense system. A *missile* is the name we give to an armed rocket—one that carries a warhead or bomb. Today, there are intercontinental ballistic missiles (ICBM's) that can carry a powerful warhead halfway around the world and deliver it exactly on target.

But more in line with the hopes and dreams of Doctor Goddard, we have incredibly complex and powerful rockets designed to take us to the moon and the other planets, and perhaps even to another solar system.

# How Rockets
# and Missiles Fly

3 . . . 2 . . . 1 . . . *FIRE!* Then a tremendous roar. For a split-second the rocket seems to hesitate. A great sheet of flame rushes from the tail, and the rocket pushes away from its launch pad. It moves at first as if in slow motion, struggling against the pull of Earth's gravity. It surges upward, gaining speed, a trail of hot flames streaking behind. Soon it is only a speck in the sky, and then it has disappeared from sight.

Rockets and missiles can go farther and much faster than any other form of transportation on Earth. Yet, like a car or a motorboat or an airplane, they are powered

76

by an engine. Fuel is fed into the engine and burned. The burning of fuel in the engine makes energy. This energy is the power which moves the vehicle.

Rockets have either a *liquid fuel* engine or a *solid fuel* engine. In both types of engine, the fuel is a combination of chemicals.

In a liquid fuel engine, the fuel is combined with an *oxidizer* (a chemical which adds oxygen to the fuel). Both the fuel and the oxidizer are carried in separate tanks or compartments in the rocket. Through tubes, they are pumped into a *combustion chamber*. There the fuel burns fiercely. As it burns, hot gases rush out the rear of the rocket through what is called a *thrust chamber*.

The hot gases rushing out of the rear of the rocket create a strong force. The blast of the hot gases in one direction creates a force pushing in the opposite direction. This is what causes the rocket to move forward. It is a *counterforce*, which we call *thrust*.

The more powerful the force of hot gases rushing out the rear of a rocket, the more powerful the thrust will be. Larger rockets need a very powerful thrust to be able to lift their heavy cargo and surge away from the Earth's gravity.

A solid fuel rocket, like a liquid fuel rocket, also uses a combination of chemicals. The chemicals, however, are mixed before they are loaded onto the rocket. A fuel is combined with an oxidizer and certain other chemicals. A mixer churns them together. After the mixing, the fuel is a gooey, syrup-like mass. It is poured into the rocket's engine case and allowed to "age" for several days. It slowly becomes a rubbery substance, called a *solid fuel.*

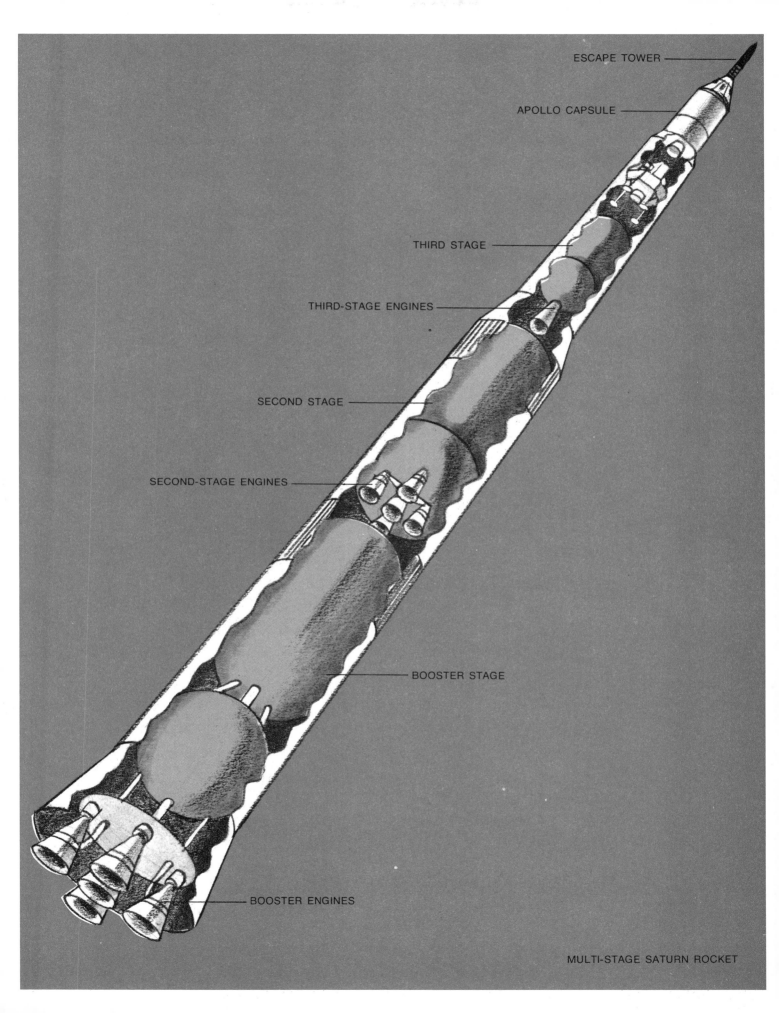

ESCAPE TOWER

APOLLO CAPSULE

THIRD STAGE

THIRD-STAGE ENGINES

SECOND STAGE

SECOND-STAGE ENGINES

BOOSTER STAGE

BOOSTER ENGINES

MULTI-STAGE SATURN ROCKET

Solid fuels cannot be regulated like liquid fuels. The flow of liquid fuels can be controlled. But a solid fuel burns steadily until it has burned itself out.

Some day scientists will develop atomic engines which will use nuclear power. A tremendous amount of energy can be produced from a very small amount of fuel in an atomic engine. This, of course, will be a great help for distant journeys deep into outer space.

Multi-stage rockets are used for extra power and speed. All of the rockets which are used for space exploration are multi-stage rockets. The first stage of a multi-stage rocket is released when it burns out. The next stage gives the rocket additional thrust. If a rocket is traveling 10,000 miles per hour when the first stage burns out, and the thrust produced by the second stage is also equal to 10,000 miles per hour, the rocket's speed will go up to 20,000 miles per hour.

Flights into outer space require a great deal of team-work. Scientists and engineers must develop the engines and guidance systems. Maintenance people check and recheck the operation of even the smallest instrument. Astronauts must be trained. But the work is going on, and man is making giant strides in exploring outer space.

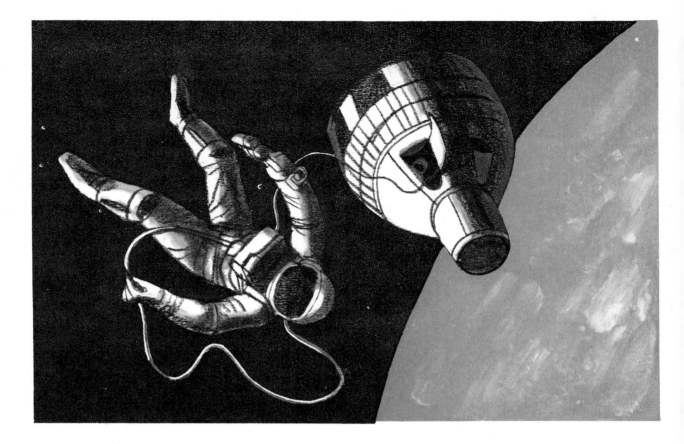

# Satellites and Space Exploration

THE GREAT AGE of space exploration has begun. Travel in outer space is no longer a dream. American astronauts and Russian cosmonauts have already orbited the Earth many times. Space vehicles have safely landed on the moon and the planet Venus.

Great advances have been made since the day in 1957 when the Russians successfully launched the first man-made satellite into orbit around the Earth. It was on October 4, 1957, that *Sputnik I*, a 184-pound sphere, was sent up. Four months later, on January 31, 1958, the United States launched *Explorer I*.

Now there are many different types of space vehicles. All, of course, are powered by rockets. A *satellite* is simply an object which orbits around a planet or sun. Our moon, in fact, is called a satellite. There are also *space probes.* A space probe does not go into orbit. Instead it soars out into space toward the moon, other planets or the sun. *Mariner III,* which traveled out past Mars, was a space probe launched by the United States. Space probes later take up an orbit, usually around the sun.

Each space vehicle has a definite purpose. A satellite carrying astronauts into space may be testing the extreme conditions that man will face in space travel. Scientists study the effects of the tremendous pressure on man as the powerful rocket ship blasts off. We experience a little of this pressure when an automobile starts quickly and we are pressed back against the seat. Scientists also need to know how a man will react to the fantastic speeds at which rockets travel. And, of course, there is *weightlessness* — man floats like a balloon in space because there is no gravity. These and many other things must be studied before space travel for us is possible.

Unmanned satellites serve many different functions. Weather or *meteorological* satellites take photographs of cloud formations and measure frontal movements.

Other unmanned satellites receive radio and television signals from Earth and transmit them back. These are *communications* satellites. They are like a giant transmitting tower 200 miles high. They can receive the television signals of a parade in Moscow and relay them back to us in the United States. This allows us to watch the parade on television as it is actually happening.

*Astronomical* satellites are giant telescopes in space which can observe and photograph the other heavenly bodies far better than any telescopes on Earth. Other satellites photograph the physical characteristics of the Earth.

Space probes, on the other hand, often investigate conditions far out in space. They take photographs and measure conditions of other planets. This information, which we could not ordinarily find out from Earth, is then sent back to us. Venus 4, the famous Russian space probe which made a soft-landing on Venus, measured the temperature there. We had thought the temperature on Venus was similar to ours on Earth. Venus 4 found it to be over 500 degrees. Venus 4 also measured the atmosphere of Venus and found very little oxygen. Because of this, it was concluded that no life like that found on Earth could survive on Venus. Space probes are actually the forerunners of the space vehicles that will take man to the moon and other planets.

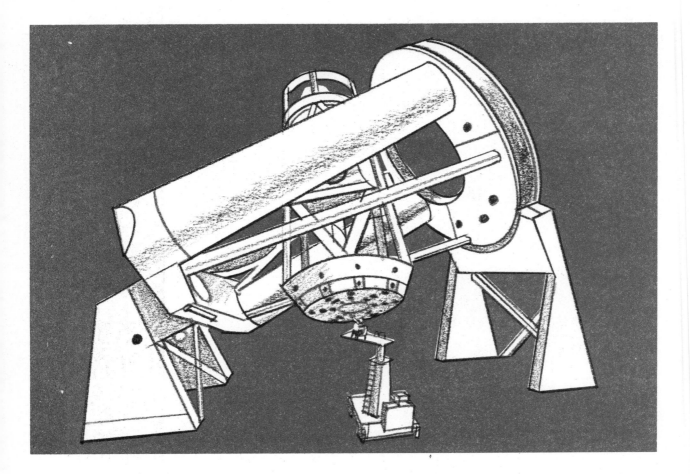

# Neighbors in Space

YEARS AGO, PEOPLE WROTE stories about space travel, but few of them really believed the idea. Most of these stories were about life on Venus or Mars. These planets are our closest neighbors. It was easiest for people to imagine that there was life on the planets nearest the Earth.

Then astronomers began to find out just how big the universe really is. Many people think of outer space as just a dark bowl-shaped sky full of cold glittering stars. Actually the stars are far from cold. They are glowing balls of heat, just like our sun.

Soon scientists began to think that *many* stars must have planets around them. Let's take just our own corner of the universe — our *galaxy*. The Milky Way Galaxy has billions and billions of stars (or suns) in it. Some scientists think that as many as 50 billion of these stars may have planets circling around them. Some of these stars may have just two or three planets, or nine planets like our solar system, or perhaps even hundreds of planets.

Of course, all the possible solar systems are not in our galaxy. There are millions of other galaxies throughout the universe. Each of these galaxies has billions of stars, too. Scientists know very little about the stars in other galaxies because they are so far away. But they think that many of those stars are suns, too, and probably have planets revolving around them.

This is why many scientists today think that there must be life somewhere else — because there are so many "somewhere elses." It would be *harder* to believe that the earth is the only place where there are living things.

If there *are* living things somewhere else in the universe, where are they? And what are they like?

These are the two big questions that no one can answer yet. Writers and TV programs have shown "creatures from outer space" with twelve arms or striped tentacles or antennae on their heads. Such things *could* be true, because twelve arms or green skin or three eyes might be very handy for living on certain kinds of planets!

On earth, plants and animals need oxygen and water and sunlight to stay alive. On some other planet, circling around some other sun, creatures might need very

different things to stay alive. Scientists do not expect to find another world exactly like ours.

Our Earth itself has changed greatly over millions and billions of years. During all those years, there have been many kinds of living things here.

This is another thing to remember in thinking about living things on other worlds. We might find another planet where life was just beginning. There might be tiny plants or animals that we could see only through a microscope, just as there were on earth billions of years ago. Or we might find a planet where all living things lived in the sea. Or one where the only living things were plants, not animals.

Any of these kinds of outer space life are possible, of course. But they are not what we hope to find. We like to think that someday we will find another planet where there is *intelligent* life. We hope to find living creatures who would be able to think and talk or communicate with us in some way. They might even be much more advanced than people on earth are.

These *intelligent* outer space creatures will have to be able to do certain things — or we will never be able to meet them. They have to be able to think about things and build things. They will be able to move around. Maybe they will fly above the surface of their planet, or move on little wheels, or run on sixteen legs! But they will have to move and to have something they can use the way we use our hands.

Any creature that will communicate across space will have to be able to build very complicated machines. And even a very smart tree couldn't do that because it has

no "hands." Probably fish or water creatures couldn't build machines either.

So the "friends" we may find on another planet will be like us in that way, at least. They will also have to have something like our eyes and ears and fingers, to help them sense and understand the things around them. But on planets with strange and different things to see and hear and touch, these senses could be very different.

Right now, we "Earthlings" still do not have a good way to talk to anybody on another planet. Our radio beams are not strong enough to travel across billions of miles of space. Our space ships and rockets cannot travel fast enough to reach another star.

Probably our first way of contacting space neighbors will be radio. Scientists are working hard on building better radio equipment. Even when we can make a very strong radio beam, though, we will not know in what direction to send our messages. We still do not know *where* in the galaxy or the universe there may be someone to receive the message. So we are also working to build huge radio *receivers*. These are great bowls that can pick up very faint, faraway radio signals.

From where? From whom?

From those intelligent outer space creatures that we think might be somewhere in our galaxy or in our universe. If we are curious about them, chances are that they are just as curious about us! They can do all the things we talked about — move around, sense things, build things, think about things.

To do all these things takes *curiosity*. And, just like us, these intelligent, curious creatures would probably begin to wonder if they were all alone in the universe. These faraway neighbors may be more advanced than we are. Perhaps their telescopes and radio beams are strong enough to reach across billions of miles of space.

Many scientists think that other planets may be trying to reach us in other ways. So they have built huge radio-telescopes that listen for messages from outer space — just a few *blips* or *bleeps* arranged in a special pattern that could not be an accident.

Perhaps, on some planet circling a faraway star, someone has looked through a powerful telescope. This creature has seen another bright star with nine small planets spinning around it. The first one is tiny and very close to the sun-star. The second is covered with thick clouds. But the third planet is blue, with a thin circle of atmosphere around it.

So someone — or something — on that far planet pushes a button. The first message starts across billions of space-miles, to let listeners on earth know that we do have neighbors in the universe!

# Will You Travel in Space?

TRAVEL IN OUTER SPACE is going to be quite different from any form of travel we have on Earth.

You will wear a special outfit—a pressure suit. This is to help your body withstand the tremendous pressures of take-off and re-entry. There are also strong pressures when the spacecraft accelerates and decelerates (speeds up and slows down). The pressure suit will also keep your body at a comfortable, steady temperature. Temperatures in outer space may vary from boiling hot to freezing cold, and they may change very suddenly, even when you aren't expecting it.

You will probably board a powerful but short-range rocket. The rocket will have to be powerful enough to surge away from the Earth's gravity. But it will be small because it will only be making a short trip of perhaps a few thousand miles. The sliding doors will close and be sealed to maintain the pressurized cabin. You will be securely strapped into a seat.

The tremendous pressure of the blast-off pins you to the back of your seat. The rocket will surge away from the Earth. It will reach a speed in orbit of somewhere around 18,000 miles an hour, very slow for travel in outer space. Your destination will be a large space station orbiting around the Earth.

As you are speeding toward a rendezvous with the space station, you will be able to see the great curve of the Earth from your cabin window. The Earth will look like a greenish-blue ball and you will be able to distinguish the outlines of continents and oceans.

The rocket will maneuver in and dock at the space station. There you will leave the craft and board another rocket ship. The size of this space ship will depend on where you are going. If it is only to the moon, it will probably be a small space ship. If your destination is another planet, it will be a much larger vehicle.

The blast-off from the space station would not really be a blast-off at all. There would be no gravity to fight against, and the spacecraft would streak off into space. It may reach speeds of hundreds of thousands of miles an hour. However, you will not feel the speed. The only sense of movement you will have is when the rocket ship speeds up or slows down. When the speed is constant or steady, it will be as if you were standing still.

The powerful engines of the rocket will not be heard. Inside the cabin the only noises will be from instruments and equipment inside the spacecraft.

Travel in a spacecraft will present special problems. You will be weightless. When you unstrap yourself from the seat, you could float through the cabin like a feather. Therefore, you will be wearing special shoes. The soles of the shoes may be coated with an adhesive so they stick to the floor. You will be able to walk but it will be like walking across flypaper — one foot lifted at a time.

Dinner will not be served by a smiling stewardess, who places a tray in front of you. If she did, it would float right off the tray. You would even have to chase your water around the cabin. Instead you will eat pre-processed foods from something like a toothpaste tube, and you will drink only through a straw.

You will have to be very careful as you move about the cabin. If you turned a door handle, you might very well turn a complete cartwheel. Trying to turn a bolt with a wrench might result in your doing a somersault. There is no gravity to keep you down, and when you exert a force one way, the opposite force could flip you completely over.

When you reach the moon or another planet, you will probably have to change space ships again at another space station. Or perhaps the capsule in which you are riding will detach itself from the body of the rocket ship. The rocket ship will stay in orbit and only the capsule will take you to your destination.

But you will be on your way — traveling in outer space. It will be an exciting trip, and you may very well be taking it some day.